T5-AFQ-493

XAMonline, Inc.
25 First Street, Suite 106
Cambridge, MA 02141
Toll Free: 1-800-509-4128
Email: info@xamonline.com
Web: www.xamonline.com
Fax: 1-617-583-5552

Library of Congress Cataloging-in-Publication Data

Wynne, Sharon A.
    MTTC Basic Skills 96 Practice Test 2: Teacher Certification /
    Sharon A. Wynne. -1st ed.
    ISBN: 978-1-60787-222-1
    1. MTTC Basic Skills 96 Practice Test 2
    2. Study Guides   3. MTTC   4. Teachers' Certification & Licensure
    5. Careers

Disclaimer:
The opinions expressed in this publication are the sole works of XAMonline and were created independently from the National Education Association, Educational Testing Service, or any State Department of Education, National Evaluation Systems or other testing affiliates.

Between the time of publication and printing, state specific standards as well as testing formats and website information may change that is not included in part or in whole within this product. Sample test questions are developed by XAMonline and reflect similar content as on real tests; however, they are not former tests. XAMonline assembles content that aligns with state standards but makes no claims nor guarantees teacher candidates a passing score. Numerical scores are determined by testing companies such as NES or ETS and then are compared with individual state standards. A passing score varies from state to state.

Printed in the United States of America   œ-1

MTTC Basic Skills 96 Practice Test 2
ISBN: 978-1-60787-222-1

READING

Directions: Read the following passage and answer questions 1–8.

Spiders can be found in almost all areas of the world with one exception, the polar regions, which are too cold for the spiders to exist. The habitats that most spiders live in, however, are the woodlands, grasslands, or forests where the insect population is high and allows spiders to catch them for food. Of course, spiders are also found in people's homes, but we don't often think about them because out of sight, out of mind, and spiders like to keep to themselves and often stay pretty well hidden. Surprisingly enough, some spiders even live on water! The water spider lives in slow moving or still water. Another water spider—the raft spider—lives in marshy places and can actually run across the surface of the water.

1. **What is the main idea of the passage?**
   (Average)

   A. Each type of spider has a certain quality or characteristic

   B. Spiders live in many different areas around the world

   C. It is difficult to find spiders because they like to keep to themselves

   D. One type of spider is know as the raft spider and can run across water

2. **Why did the author write this article?**
   (Average)

   A. To entertain

   B. To persuade

   C. To describe

   D. To inform

3. **What is the best summary of this paragraph?**
   (Rigorous)

   A. Spiders reside in various habitats except for areas of extreme cold. They can even be found on water

   B. Spiders live in areas where the insect population is high so they can survive

   C. Spiders fit the saying, "out of sight, out of mind," because they are very private insects

   D. Spiders that run across the water are also known as raft spiders

4. **How is the passage above organized?**
   (Average)

   A. Sequence of events

   B. Compare and contrast

   C. Statement support

   D. Cause and effect

5. **What comparison is made in the paragraph?**
   (Rigorous)

   A. Arctic spiders to woodland spiders

   B. People and spiders

   C. Woodland spiders and water spiders

   D. The arctic region to the woodland areas

6. **What is the author implying by using the words *surprisingly enough*?**
   (Rigorous)

   A. She is scared of spiders that are able to live in the water

   B. She always thought that spiders were strictly land lubbers

   C. She thought they always stayed well-hidden, and water surfaces are not well-hidden

   D. She thinks that spiders are brought out into the water by rafts

7. **What words does the author use to clarify information for the reader?**
(Average)

A. Actually

B. Another water spider

C. Raft spider

D. Surprisingly enough

8. **What would have been the best transition word for the author to use to connect these two sentences?**
(Easy)

Surprisingly enough, some spiders even live on water! The water spider lives in slow moving or still water.

A. Then,

B. Beyond,

C. For example,

D. Immediately,

9. **What does the word *meander* mean in the sentence below?**
(Easy)

Michael was taking a long time to return to his seat after sharpening his pencil at the back of the room. After leaving the sharpener, he meandered around the room before eventually making his way back to his own seat.

A. rolled

B. roamed

C. slithered

D. stomped

10. **What does the word *interject* mean in the sentence below?**
(Easy)

Nancy was speaking with her best friend Sierra. Nancy's little sister was standing nearby and was eavesdropping on their conversation. Suddenly, she heard something that interested her and had to interject her opinion about the subject the girls were talking about.

A. repeat

B. pierce

C. intersect

D. state

11. When reading the book *Stormbreaker* by Anthony Horowitz the reader feels like they are a part of the action. The author uses so many details to bring the reader into the setting of story and this puts the reader right beside Alex Rider, the main character in the story.

    Is this a valid or invalid argument?
    (Average)

    A. Valid

    B. Invalid

12. Let's go see the movie *Alice in Wonderland.* It's a great movie and is Johnny Depp is awesome!

    Is this a valid or invalid argument?
    (Average)

    A. Valid

    B. Invalid

13. Which sentence in the passage below is irrelevant?
    (Rigorous)

    Davy Crockett grew up in Tennessee. When he was just a young boy he learned to hunt, fish, and drive cattle. At twelve years old, he traveled three hundred miles to complete a cattle drive. Davy's father thought school was important, but Davy did not agree. He left home and did not return until he was fifteen. He had grown to nearly six feet tall. When he returned, he was employed by a farmer whose son taught school. It was because of this fact that Davy developed a new interest in reading and writing. Davy also developed another interest—shooting rifles and hunting animals. He often missed his mother. Legend has it that Davy had very good aim and captured more than 100 bears in just a six-month period.

    A. Davy Crockett grew up in Tennessee

    B. When he was just a young boy he learned to hunt, fish, and drive cattle

    C. He had grown to nearly six-feet tall

    D. Legend has it that Davy had very good aim

14. **Which sentence in the passage above is irrelevant?**
(Rigorous)

A. Davy also developed another interest

B. He often missed his mother

C. Legend has it that Davy had very good aim

D. Davy captured more than 100 bears in just six months

15. **Boys are smarter than girls. Is this sentence fact or opinion?**
(Easy)

A. Fact

B. Opinion

16. **Turkey burgers are better than beef burgers. Is this sentence fact or opinion?**
(Easy)

A. Fact

B. Opinion

17. **Johnny Depp stars in the movie *Charlie and the Chocolate Factory*. Is this sentence fact or opinion?**
(Easy)

A. Fact

B. Opinion

18. **We live at 5310 Fair Oaks Drive in Chicago, Illinois. Is this sentence fact or opinion?**
(Easy)

A. Fact

B. Opinion

19. **What conclusion can be drawn from the passage below?**
(Rigorous)

When she walked into the room she gasped in disbelief as her hands rose to her face and her eyes bulged large. After she picked her jaw up off the floor, a huge smile spread across her face as her best friend came up and wrapped her arms around her and wished her a happy birthday.

A. The girl didn't know anyone in the room

B. The girl saw something shocking

C. The girl was being thrown a surprise party

D. The girl got punched in the face

20. **What conclusion can be drawn from the paragraph below?** *(Average)*

Joel stood at the water's edge staring into the waves as his legs trembled violently. His mind flashed back to last summer and his entire body joined his legs and began to tremble. He tried to even his breathing as he took slow deep breaths before deciding to head into the surf.

A. The water was really cold

B. Joel saw a shark in the water

C. Last summer was better than this summer

D. Joel is afraid of the water because something happened

Directions: Read the following passage and answer questions 21–24.

Deciding which animal to get as the family pet can be a very difficult decision and there are many things to take into consideration. First, you must consider the size of your home and the area that will be dedicated to the pet. If your home is a smaller one, then you probably want to get a small dog or even a cat. If you are lucky enough to have larger home with plenty of room inside and out, then most certainly consider a large or even a more active breed of dog. One other thing to is how often and how long you are outside of the home. Cats do not need to be let out to relieve themselves. They are normally trained to use a litter box. On the other hand, dogs require being let out. Dogs also require more exercise than cats and often need to be walked. This can be aggravating to an owner especially on rainy days. Therefore, when deciding which pet is best for your family, it is necessary to consider more than whether or not you want a dog or a cat, but which animal will best fit into your family's lifestyle.

21. **How does the author feel about dogs?**
(Rigorous)

   A. The author likes dogs and cats the same

   B. The author thinks that dogs are aggravating

   C. The author believes they require more care than cats

   D. The author feels that dogs are more active than cats

22. **How does the author feel about the size of people's houses?**
(Rigorous)

   A. The author believes that people with larger homes are lucky

   B. The author thinks that if you have a small house you should have a cat

   C. The author feels that only people with large homes should own animals

   D. The author thinks that only those who own homes should own pets

23. **From this passage, one can infer that:**
(Rigorous)

   A The author owns a cat

   B More people own dogs than cats

   C Cats are smarter than dogs

   D The author owns a dog

24. **From this passage, one can infer that:**
(Rigorous)

   A. Either a dog or cat will be right for every family who wants a pet

   B. Choosing a pet is not solely one family member's job

   C. Only someone who enjoys exercising should get a dog

   D. Big dogs will not survive in a small house

Directions: Read the following passage and answer questions 25–31.

According to Factmonster.com, the most popular Internet activity is sending and/or reading email. Approximately 92% of Internet users report using the Internet for this purpose. 89% of Internet users report that they use the Internet to search for information. Two popular search engines are Google and Yahoo! The introduction of the Internet has made it easy to gather and research information quickly. Other reasons that Internet users use the Internet is to search for driving directions, look into a hobby or interest, or research a product or service before buying, just to name a few. Creative <u>enterprises</u> such as remixing songs or lyrics stood at the bottom of reasons people use the Internet. Surprisingly, only 11% of Internet users said they use the Internet for creative purposes. Perhaps people are using specific software to be creative. Where do you rank? Think about why you last used the Internet.

25. **What is the main idea of the passage?**
(Average)

A. Factmonster has a lot of great facts for people to research

B. People use the Internet for a variety of reasons

C. The main reason the Internet is used is to check emails

D. People aren't as creative as they used to be before the Internet

26. **Why did the author write this article?**
(Average)

A To convince the reader to use the Internet

B To teach the reader how use the Internet

C To encourage the reader to use the Internet

D To inform the reader about Internet usage trends

27. **How is the passage above organized?**
(Average)

A. Sequence of events

B. Cause and effect

C. Statement support

D. Compare and contrast

28. **What cause and effect relationship exists in this paragraph?**
(Rigorous)

   A. The U.S. postal service is suffering from the introduction of email

   B. Google and Yahoo! are used most often to search information

   C. The introduction of the Internet has made gathering information easy

   D. People are less creative since they aren't using their computers for this reason

29. **By using the word *surprisingly* in the passage, what is the author implying?**
(Rigorous)

   A. It is thought that the Internet is used more creative purposes

   B. People are thought to be more creative than they really are

   C. It is thought that fewer than 11% would use the Internet for creative purposes

   D. Software companies are making 11% more creative software

30. **Which transition word could the author have used to connect these two sentence?**
(Average)

Approximately 92% of Internet users report using the Internet for this purpose. 89% of Internet users report that they use the Internet to search for information.

   A. Additionally,

   B. Therefore,

   C. Next,

   D. Similarly,

31. **What does the word *enterprises* mean in the passage?**
(Average)

   A. people

   B. endeavors

   C. businesses

   D. musicians

Directions: Read the following passage and answer questions 32–34.

The poems both use personification to bring the subjects of the poem to life. Both poems were also very entertaining. In <u>The Subway</u> the author says that the subway, also known as a dragon, swallows up the people and then spits them out at the next stop. Similarly, in the poem <u>Steam Shovel</u>, the author says that the steam shovel chews up the dirt that it scoops up and smiles amiably at the people below.

The subjects of the poems are compared to different things. The subway is compared to a dragon with green scales. Dragons breathe fire. The steam shovel is compared to an ancient dinosaur with a long neck and dripping jaws.

32. **How is the above passage organized?**
    (Average)

    A. Compare and contrast

    B. Cause and effect

    C. Sequence of events

    D. Statement support

33. **Which sentence in the passage above is irrelevant?**
    (Average)

    A. Both poems were also very entertaining

    B. The subway is also known as a dragon

    C. The subway swallows people up and spits them out

    D. The author says that the steam shovel chews up the dirt

34. **Which sentence in the passage above is irrelevant?**
    (Rigorous)

    A. The subjects of the poems are compared to different things.

    B. The subway is compared to a dragon with green scales.

    C. Dragons breathe fire.

    D. The steam shovel is compared to an ancient dinosaur.

Directions: Read the following passage and answer questions 35–36.

Have you ever wondered what chewing gum is made from? What it is that allows us to chew it for hours without ever disintegrating? Chicle is a gum, or sap, that comes from the sapodilla tree. The sapodilla tree is an American tropical evergreen that is native to South Florida. Flavorings, corn syrup, and sugar or artificial sweeteners are other ingredients that go into the production of chewing gum. Legend has it that Native Americans chewed spruce resin to quench their thirst. Today, gum is chewed for many reasons by many different groups of people.

35. **What conclusion can be drawn from the above passage?**
   (Rigorous)

   A. Everyone in South Florida has heard of the sapodilla tree

   B. Many people have wondered what makes gum chewy

   C. Some type of sweetener is used in gum production

   D. Native Americans invented gum

36. **What can be inferred from the passage?**
   (Rigorous)

   A. The gum *Chiclets* took its name from the ingredient Chicle used in gum

   B. Gum is disgusting after its been chewed for a few hours

   C. Gum is only made in the United States because that's where the sapodilla tree grows

   D. When someone is thirsty they should chew gum

Directions: Read the following passage and answer questions 37–40.

The word *cycle* comes from the Greek word *kyklos*, which means circle or wheel. There are many different types of cycles. The word *unicycle* comes from the prefix *uni-*, which means "one," combined with the root *cycle.* When the prefix and root word cycle are combined, it creates a word that means one circle or wheel. Unicycles are often used for entertainment rather than exercise.

A suffix *bi-* means "two," which when combined with the word cycle, creates the word bicycle. How many wheels does a bicycle have? Many young children ride a tricycle because it has three wheels and is easy to ride. The prefix *tri-* means "three," and when it is combined with the root word *cycle* the new word is "three wheels." It is even possible to make the word *motorcycle.* Once you know how to use <u>roots</u>, it is easy to figure out the meaning of an unknown word.

37. **What is the main idea of the passage?**
    (Average)

    A. There are many types of cycles

    B. The prefix *uni-* means one

    C. Words can be defined by its parts

    D. Unicycles are often used for entertainment

38. **What does the word *roots* mean?**
    (Easy)

    A. Stable parts of plants

    B. Where one originated

    C. The base portion of a word

    D. A spelling tool

39. **Which is an opinion contained in this passage?**
    (Average)

    A. Once you know how to use roots, it is easy to figure out the meaning of an unknown word

    B. Many young children ride a tricycle

    C. Unicycles are often used for entertainment rather than exercise

    D. The word cycle comes from the Greek word *kyklos*

40. **From this article you can see that the author thinks:**
(Rigorous)

    A. Riding a bicycle is good exercise

    B. It is important to know about the English language

    C. Cycle is a confusing word

    D. It is more important to understand the prefixes and suffixes

WRITING

Directions: Read the sentences and decide whether any of the underlined parts contains a grammatical construction, a word use, or an instance of incorrect or omitted punctuation or capitalization that would be inappropriate in carefully written English.

1. **It will <u>definitely</u> be a great time and I am <u>positively</u> that everyone <u>who</u> attends will enjoy the party.**
   (Average)

   A. definite

   B. positive

   C. whom

   D. No change is necessary

2. **There are <u>many</u> different <u>activities</u> planned for the day in all of the surrounding <u>communitys</u>.**
   (Average)

   A. much

   B. activitys

   C. communities

   D. No change is necessary

3. **Jordan accepted <u>Chrises</u> invitation to go with him to the dance on Friday night.**
   (Rigorous)

   A. Chris's

   B. Chris'

   C. Chrises'

   D. No change is necessary

4. **Michelle <u>was trying</u> to do her homework, but <u>he was making</u> too much noise.**
   (Rigorous)

   A. tried

   B. her brother

   C. made

   D. No change is necessary

5. **When I returned home after running errands for the past hour, I wondered <u>whose</u> car was parked in my driveway.**
   (Rigorous)

   A. who's

   B. who is

   C. whos

   D. No change is necessary

6. The expectations that have been put on <u>teachers</u> in the past few years <u>have grown</u> and <u>they</u> are very difficult to manage.
(Rigorous)

A. teacher's

B. has grown

C. these expectations

D. No change is necessary

7. Austin <u>was watching</u> television on the couch when his dad <u>looked</u> at him with an encouraging look. "I <u>has taken</u> out the trash already," Austin said.
(Average)

A. had watched

B. looking

C. have taken

D. Not change necessary

8. <u>Christian Montgomery</u> <u>our honorable mayor</u> will be leading us in the <u>ceremonies</u> that day.
(Rigorous)

A. Christian montgomery

B. Montgomery, our honorable mayor,

C. Ceremonies

D. No change is necessary

9. Pizza tastes <u>more better</u> when you <u>put</u> <u>cheese</u>, mushrooms, and onions all over the top of it.
(Easy)

A. better

B. putt

C. cheesy

D. No change is necessary

10. The lemonade that <u>was being</u> sold at the <u>children's</u> lemonade stand was <u>more sweet</u> than the iced tea.
(Rigorous)

A. has been

B. childrens

C. sweeter

D. No change is necessary

11. The <u>students</u> and the <u>teachers</u> <u>is</u> going to attend the performance at noon on Thursday.
(Easy)

A. student's

B. teachers'

C. are

D. No change is necessary

12. After the town was evacuated <u>due to</u> expected strong <u>storms,</u> I reported to the authorities that there <u>wasn't nobody</u> left in our whole house.
(Average)

A. because of

B. storms I...

C. wasn't anybody

D. No change is necessary

13. This weekend we are going to <u>mow</u> the <u>lawn, wash</u> the windows and <u>trimming</u> the shrubs.
(Easy)

A. mowing

B. lawn; wash

C. trim

D. No change is necessary

14. The local meteorologists <u>are</u> forecasting <u>neither</u> rain <u>or</u> snow for the holiday week.
(Rigorous)

A. is

B. niether

C. nor

D. No change is necessary

15. We will <u>be celebrating</u> the <u>Fourth of July</u> at <u>independence park</u> located in the center of Gorham Township.
(Average)

A. celebrating

B. fourth of July

C. Independence Park

D. No change is necessary

Directions: In each of the following sentences, some part of the sentence or the entire sentence is underlined. Beneath each sentence you will find four ways of writing the underlined part. Select the best answer that will make the sentence correct.

16. <u>The states of Oklahoma, Texas and Missouri were severe affected by the drought caused from a lack of rain this summer.</u>
(Average)

    A. The states of Oklahoma, Texas and Missouri were more severely affected by the drought caused from a lack of rain this summer.

    B. The states of Oklahoma, Texas and Missouri was severely affected by the drought caused from a lack of rain this summer.

    C. The states of Oklahoma, Texas and Missouri were severely affected by the drought caused from a lack of rain this summer.

    D. No change is necessary

17. <u>Who do you think has the neatest handwriting in the class?</u>
(Rigorous)

    A. Whom do you think have the neater handwriting in the class?

    B. Who do you think have the neatest handwriting in the class?

    C. Who do you think has the neatest handwriting in the class.

    D. No change is necessary

18. **The professor and his assistant presented they're report at the annual conference of financial economic stimulus representatives.**
(Average)

A. The professor and his assistant presented its report at the annual conference of financial economic stimulus representatives.

B. The professor and his assistant presented theirs report at the annual conference of financial economic stimulus representatives.

C. The professor and his assistant presented their report at the annual conference of financial economic stimulus representatives.

D. No change is necessary

19. **Since its supposed to rain today I think its best if you take your umbrella.**
(Average)

A. Since it's supposed to rain today, I think its best if you take you're umbrella.

B. Since it's supposed to rain today, I think it's best if you take your umbrella.

C. Since its supposed to rain today I think its best if you take you're umbrealla.

D. No change is necessary

20. **Our regularly scheduled meeting will be hold on Tuesday, March 11 at 3:00 that afternoon.**
(Easy)

A. Our regular scheduled meeting will be hold on Tuesday, March 11 at 3:00 in the afternoon.

B. Our regularly scheduled meeting will be held on Tuesday, March 11 at 3:00 in the afternoon.

C. Are regularly scheduled meeting will be held on Tuesday, March 11 at 3:00 that afternoon.

D. No change is necessary

21. <u>**The frog eggs were laid a few weeks ago, so they have been hatching soon.**</u>
(Easy)

A. The frog eggs were laid a few weeks ago, so they will be hatching soon.

B. The frog eggs were laid a few weeks ago, so they is hatching soon.

C. The frog eggs were laid a few weeks ago, so they be done hatching soon.

D. No change is necessary

22. <u>**We were supposed to work on a project for school, but after an hour we started to get hungry and deciding to make popcorn.**</u>
(Average)

A. We were supposed to work on a project for school, but after an hour we started to get hungry and were deciding to make popcorn.

B. We were supposed to work on a project for school, but after an hour we started to get hungry and decide to make popcorn.

C. We were supposed to work on a project for school, but after an hour we started to get hungry and decided to make popcorn.

D. No change is necessary

23. <u>**I had brought home some movies from the video store but not anybody wanted to watch them so we played a game instead.**</u>
(Average)

A. I brought home some movies from the video store but not anyone wanted to watch them so we played a game instead.

B. I brought home some movies from the video store but nobody wanted to watch them so we played a game instead.

C. I brought home some movies from the video store but somebody wanted to watch them so we played a game instead.

D. No change is necessary

24. **Coloring hard boiled eggs is an Easter tradition** <u>**that many people still follow today.**</u>
(Rigorous)

A. that many people followed today.
B. that many people following today.
C. that much peoples follow today.
D. No change is necessary

25. Temperatures are rising, <u>yet the trees are blooming and the grass is quickly growing.</u> *(Rigorous)*

   A. but the trees is blooming and the grass is quickly growing.

   B. and the trees are blooming and the grass is quickly growing.

   C. yet, the trees are blooming and the grass is quickly growing.

   D. No change is necessary

26. <u>In my opinion we would all be much better off if there were less choices in the grocery stores.</u> There seems to be an overabundance of choice and it is confusing to some. *(Rigorous)*

   A. In my opinion, we should all be much more better off is there was less choices in the grocery stores.

   B. In my opinion, we would all be better off if there were less choices in the grocery stores.

   C. In my opinion we would all be much better off if there were fewer choices in the grocery stores.

   D. No change is necessary

27. <u>Supposably, the keynote speaker at the annual convention is an alumni of Princeton University.</u> *(Average)*

   A. Supposedly, the keynote speaker at the annual convention is an alumni of Princeton University.

   B. Supposably the keynote speaker, at the annual convention, is an alumni of Princeton University.

   C. Supposably, the keynote speaker during the annual convention was an alumnus at Princeton University.

   D. No change is necessary

28. <u>I was not expecting to except his advice but it actually made sense and solved the problem.</u> *(Rigorous)*

   A. I was not expecting to except his advise, but it actually made sense and solved the problem.

   B. I was not expecting to accept his advice but it actually made sense and solved the problem.

   C. I was not expecting to except his advice since it actually made sense and solved the problem.

   D. No change is necessary

29. **When children are learning to read, they often read allowed in order to assist with monitoring their own comprehension.**
(Average)

   A. When children is learning to read, we often read allowed in order to assist with monitoring their own comprehension.

   B. When children are learning to read, they often read aloud in order to assist with monitoring their own comprehension.

   C. When children are learning to read, she often read allowed in order to assist with monitor there own comprehension.

   D. No change is necessary

30. **Many northern residents are choosing to immigrate to the south to take advantage of lower taxes and nicer weather.**
(Rigorous)

   A. Many Northern residents are choosing to immigrate to the South to take advantage of lower taxes and nicer weather.

   B. Many northern residents choosed to immigrate to the south to take advantage of lower taxes and nicer weather.

   C. Many northern residents are choosing to emigrate to the south to take advantage of lower taxes and nicer weather.

   D. No change is necessary

31. **When I was younger, my family and I used to go to visit my grandparents for the summer at their home in North Carolina.**
(Rigorous)

   A. When I was younger, my family and I use to go to visit my grandparents for the summer at their home in North Carolina.

   B. When I was younger, my family and me used to go to visit my Grandparent's for the summer at their home in North Carolina.

   C. When I was younger my family and us used to go to visit my grandparents for the summer at there home in North Carolina.

   D. No change is necessary

32. **Maurice put together a good presentation in class and he did good.**
(Average)

   A. Maurice put together a good presentation in class and he did well.

   B. Maurice put together a well presentation in class and he did well.

   C. Maurice put together a well presentation in class and he did good.

   D. No change is necessary

33. **I can't believe that you didn't see that red light that was so oblivious.**
(Easy)

   A. I can't believe that you didn't see that red light that was so enormous.

   B. I can't believe that you didn't see that red light that was so relevant.

   C. I can't believe that you didn't see that red light that was so obvious.

   D. No change is necessary

34. **My lunchbox contained many different treats; cookies, fruit, nuts, and cheese.**
(Rigorous)

   A. My lunchbox contained many different treats: cookies, fruit, nuts, and cheese.
   B. My lunchbox contained many different treats, cookies, fruit, nuts and cheese.
   C. My lunchbox contained many different treats. cookies, fruit, nuts and cheese.
   D. No change is necessary.

35. <u>**Under the bridge near the river bank many turtles sat sunning themselves.**</u>
(Average)

A. Under the bridge near the river bank, much turtles sat sunny theirselves.

B. Under the bridge, near the river bank, many turtles sat sunning themselves.

C. Under the bridge near the river bank, many turtles sat sunning themselves.

D. No change is necessary

36. <u>**I have just finished the book, "The Lion king," and I would recommend it to anyone who enjoys a good mystery.**</u>
(Average)

A. I have just finished the book *The Lion King* and I would recommend it to anyone who enjoys a good mystery.

B. I have just finished the book *the Lion King* and I would recommend it to anyone who enjoys a good mystery.

C. I have just finished the book, "the lion king" and I would recommend it to anyone who enjoys a good mystery.

D. No change is necessary

37. <u>**The rabbit was named kangaroo because it liked to jump.**</u>
(Average)

A. The Rabbit was named Kangaroo because it liked to jump.

B. The rabbit was named Kangaroo because it liked to jump.

C. The Rabbit was named kangaroo because it liked to jump.

D. No change is necessary

38. <u>**The documentary that we watched about the battle of bull run was very graphic.**</u>
(Easy)

A. The documentary that we watched about the battle of Bull Run was very graphic.

B. The documentary that we watched about the battle of Bull run was very graphic.

C. The documentary that we watched about The Battle of Bull Run was very graphic.

D. No change is necessary

Writing Essay

"Because the traditional grading scale of A through F fosters needless competition and pressure, colleges and universities should use a simple pass/fail system."

Discuss the extent to which you agree or disagree with this opinion. Support your views with specific reasons and examples from your own experience, observations, or reading.

MATH

1. **Express .0000456 in scientific notation.**
   (Average)

   A. $4.56x10^{-4}$

   B. $45.6x10^{-6}$

   C. $4.56x10^{-6}$

   D. $4.56x10^{-5}$

2. **Change $.\overline{63}$ into a fraction in simplest form.**
   (Rigorous)

   A. $63/100$

   B. $7/11$

   C. $6\ 3/10$

   D. $2/3$

3. **The digit 4 in the number 302.41 is in the**
   (Easy)

   A. Tenths place

   B. Ones place

   C. Hundredths place

   D. Hundreds place

4. **Which of the following illustrates an inverse property?**
   (Easy)
   A. $a + b = a - b$

   B. $a + b = b + a$

   C. $a + 0 = a$

   D. $a + (-a) = 0$

5. **$7t - 4 \cdot 2t + 3t \cdot 4 \div 2 =$**
   (Average)

   A. 5t

   B. 0

   C. 31t

   D. 18t

6. **If cleaning costs are $32 for 4 hours, how much is it for 10.5 hours?**
   (Average)

   A. $112.50

   B. $87

   C. $84

   D. $76.50

7. **Estimate the sum of 1498 + 1309.**
   (Average)

   A. 2900

   B. 2850

   C. 2800

   D. 2600

8. **Mr. Brown feeds his cat premium cat food, which costs $40 per month. Approximately how much will it cost to feed her for one year?**
   (Average)

   A. $500

   B. $400

   C. $80

   D. $4800

9. **A carton of milk priced at $6.00 is 30% off. Another carton priced at $5.80 is 20% off. Which one is the better buy?**
   (Rigorous)

   A. The $5.80 carton

   B. The $6.00 carton

   C. Both are equal

   D. There is not enough information

10. **What is 30% of 450?**
    (Easy)

    A. 120

    B. 135

    C. 115

    D. None of the above

11. **Joe reads 20 words/min., and Jan reads 80 words/min. How many minutes will it take Joe to read the same number of words that it takes Jan 40 minutes to read?**
    (Rigorous)

    A. 10

    B. 20

    C. 80

    D. 160

12. **Which of the following is a simple statement that can be assigned a truth value?**
    (Average)

    A. It is sunny today

    B. Please put away the books

    C. The wind blew and the leaves fell

    D. They will stay home or they will go to the mall

13. The following is an example of reasoning using:

They drove or they rode the bus.
They did not drive, therefore they rode the bus.

(Average)

A. Law of detachment

B. Law of contraposition

C. Law of syllogism

D. Disjunctive syllogism

14. Solve for x:

$3x + 5 \geq 8 + 7x$

(Average)

A. $x \geq -\frac{3}{4}$

B. $x \leq -\frac{3}{4}$

C. $x \geq \frac{3}{4}$

D. $x \leq \frac{3}{4}$

15. Solve for x:

$7 + 3x - 6 = 3x + 5 - x$

(Average)

A. 2.5

B. 4

C. 4.5

D. 27

16. Marvin bought a bag of candy. He gave half of the pieces to his friend Mike and one-third of the pieces to his sister Lisa. He ate half of the remaining pieces and had 15 left. How many pieces of candy were in the bag in the beginning?
(Rigorous)

A. 120

B. 90

C. 30

D. 180

17. A boat travels 30 miles upstream in three hours. It makes the return trip in one and a half hours. What is the speed of the boat in still water?
(Rigorous)

A. 10 mph

B. 15 mph

C. 20 mph

D. 30 mph

18. What is the next term in the sequence

$$\frac{2}{7}, \frac{13}{21}, \frac{20}{21}, \frac{9}{7}, \dots$$

(Rigorous)

A. $\dfrac{29}{21}$

B. $\dfrac{17}{21}$

C. $\dfrac{11}{7}$

D. $\dfrac{34}{21}$

19. What is the 10th term in the following sequence?

3, 6, 12, 24, …..

(Rigorous)

A. 3072

B. 1024

C. 512

D. 1536

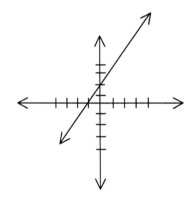

20. What is the equation of the above graph?
(Average)

A. $2x + y = 2$

B. $2x - y = -2$

C. $2x - y = 2$

D. $2x + y = -2$

21. The figure below represents the position (x), velocity (v) and acceleration (a) of a car moving in one direction as functions of time (t). According to the graph

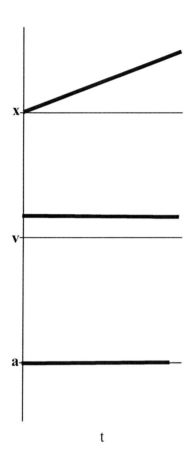

(Average)

A. The car is at rest

B. The car is moving at a fixed speed

C. The car is speeding up

D. The car changes direction in the middle

22. Which of the following shapes is a rhombus? *(Easy)*

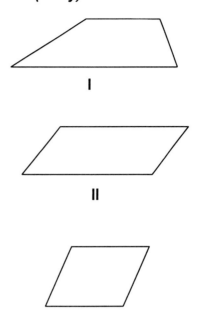

A. III

B. II

C. I

D. None of the above

23. The angles in any triangle *(Easy)*

A. Add up to 180 degrees

B. Are all equal

C. Are all right angles

D. Don't always add up to 180 degrees

24. **If a ship sails due south 6 miles, then due west 8 miles, how far was it from the starting point?**
(Average)

A. 100 miles

B. 10 miles

C. 14 miles

D. 48 miles

25. **A car is driven north at 74 miles per hour from point A. Another car is driven due east at 65 miles per hour starting from the same point at the same time. How far are the cars away from each other after 2 hours?**
(Rigorous)

A. 175.87 miles

B. 232.66 miles

C. 196.99 miles

D. 202.43 miles

26. **The mass of a cookie is closest to**
(Average)

A. 0.5 kg

B. 0.5 grams

C. 15 grams

D. 1.5 grams

27. **You have a gallon of water and remove a total of 30 ounces. How many milliliters do you have left?**
(Rigorous)

A. 2900 ml

B. 1100 ml

C. 980 ml

D. 1000 ml

28. **Seventh grade students are working on a project using non-standard measurement. Which would not be an appropriate instrument for measuring the length of the classroom?**
(Easy)

A. A student's foot

B. A student's arm span

C. A student's jump

D. All are appropriate

29.

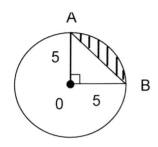

Compute the area of the shaded region, given a radius of 5 meters. 0 is the center. *(Rigorous)*

A. 7.13 cm²

B. 7.13 m²

C. 78.5 m²

D. 19.63 m²

30. Find the area of the figure pictured below.

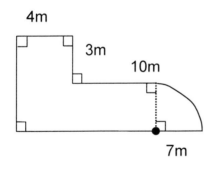

(Rigorous)

A. 136.47 m²

B. 148.48 m²

C. 293.86 m²

D. 178.47 m²

31. What conclusion can be drawn from the graph below?

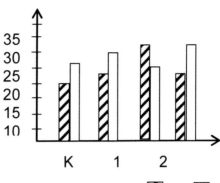

MLK Elementary Student Enrollment   Girls   Boys

(Average)

A. The number of students in first grade exceeds the number in second grade

B. There are more boys than girls in the entire school

C. There are more girls than boys in the first grade

D. Third grade has the largest number of students

32. A school band has 200 members. Looking at the pie chart below, determine which statement is true about the band.

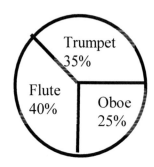

(Average)

A. There are more trumpet players than flute players

B. There are fifty oboe players in the band

C. There are forty flute players in the band

D. One-third of all band members play the trumpet

33. You wish to create a visual display showing test score trends over several decades for a school. What kind of chart would be the most suitable? *(Average)*

A. circle graph

B. bar graph

C. histogram

D. line graph

34. Which of the following statements is not true about the graph shown below?

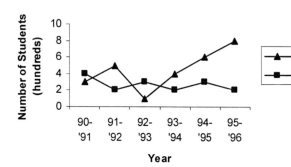

(Average)

A. Franklin school shows a rising trend in student enrollment

B. Harrison school shows a falling trend in student enrollment

C. Both schools show similar trends in student enrollment

D. Neither school has had more than 900 students

35. The stem and leaf plot below shows the heights of several children in a class in feet. What is the median height?
(Easy)

3	6 9
4	1 2 3 4 4 9
5	1 3 5

A. 4 ft

B. 4.9 ft

C. 4.4 ft

D. 5.1 ft

36. Which of these statements about the following data set is correct?

2, 5, 12, 6, 3, 9, 5, 12, 20, 2, 3, 5, 21, 12

(Rigorous)

A. There are 2 modes, the median is 8.5 and the range is 10

B. There are 2 modes, the median is 5.5 and the range is 19

C. There are 4 modes, the median is 5.5 and the range is 19

D. There are 2 modes, the median is 5.5 and the range is 10

37. Compute the median for the following data set:

{12, 19, 13, 16, 17, 14}

(Easy)

A. 14.5

B. 15.17

C. 15

D. 16

38. How many ways are there to choose a potato and two green vegetables from a choice of three potatoes and seven green vegetables?
(Rigorous)

A. 126

B. 63

C. 21

D. 252

39. How many 3 letter sequences can be formed if the first letter must always be a consonant (not a, e, i, o , u), the second letter must always be a vowel (a, e, i, o, or u), and the third letter must be different from the first.
(Rigorous)

   A. 2100

   B. 4056

   C. 3250

   D. 2625

40. Given a spinner with the numbers one through eight, what is the probability that you will not spin an even number or a number greater than four?
(Rigorous)

   A. ¼

   B. ½

   C. ¾

   D. 1

READING

Directions: Read the following passage and answer questions 1–8.

Spiders can be found in almost all areas of the world with one exception, the polar regions, which are too cold for the spiders to exist. The habitats that most spiders live in, however, are the woodlands, grasslands, or forests where the insect population is high and allows spiders to catch them for food. Of course, spiders are also found in people's homes, but we don't often think about them because out of sight, out of mind, and spiders like to keep to themselves and often stay pretty well hidden. Surprisingly enough, some spiders even live on water! The water spider lives in slow moving or still water. Another water spider—the raft spider—lives in marshy places and can actually run across the surface of the water.

1.   **What is the main idea of the passage?**
     (Average)

      A.   Each type of spider has a certain quality or characteristic

      B.   Spiders live in many different areas around the world

      C.   It is difficult to find spiders because they like to keep to themselves

      D.   One type of spider is know as the raft spider and can run across water

Answer: B. Spiders live in many different areas around the world
Choices A, C, and D are all supporting details of the main idea, "Spiders live in many different areas around the world."

2. **Why did the author write this article?**
   (Average)

   A.   To entertain

   B.   To persuade

   C.   To describe

   D.   To inform

Answer: D. To inform
The author wrote this article to teach its readers about the different types of spiders—in other words to inform them.

3. **What is the best summary of this paragraph?**
   (Rigorous)

   A.   Spiders reside in various habitats except for areas of extreme cold. They can even be found on water

   B.   Spiders live in areas where the insect population is high so they can survive

   C.   Spiders fit the saying, "out of sight, out of mind," because they are very private insects

   D.   Spiders that run across the water are also known as raft spiders

Answer: A. Spiders reside in various habitats except for areas of extreme cold. They can even be found on water
Choice A is the only choice that applies to the whole paragraph and is therefore the best summary.

4. **How is the passage above organized?**
   (Average)

      A.   Sequence of events

      B.   Compare and contrast

      C.   Statement support

      D.   Cause and effect

Answer: C. Statement support
The main idea of each paragraph is stated and then supporting sentences follow. Therefore, this is a "statement support" organization example.

5. **What comparison is made in the paragraph?**
   (Rigorous)

      A.   Arctic spiders to woodland spiders

      B.   People and spiders

      C.   Woodland spiders and water spiders

      D.   The arctic region to the woodland areas

Answer: D. The arctic region to the woodland areas
The author begins the paragraph by comparing the arctic region to the woodland region and how they are different, and therefore, not appropriate for spiders to reside.

6. **What is the author implying by using the words *surprisingly enough*? (Rigorous)**

   A.   She is scared of spiders that are able to live in the water

   B.   She always thought that spiders were strictly land lubbers

   C.   She thought they always stayed well-hidden, and water surfaces are not well-hidden

   D.   She thinks that spiders are brought out into the water by rafts

Answer: B. She always thought that spiders were strictly land lubbers
The author is implying that she is surprised that spiders can survive on the water because she thought they were strictly land creatures.

7. **What words does the author use to clarify information for the reader? (Average)**

   A.   Actually

   B.   Another water spider

   C.   Raft spider

   D.   Surprisingly enough

Answer: C. Raft spider
By placing the words "raft spider" inside of dashes, the author is defining the name of the water spider mentioned in the sentence.

8. **What would have been the best transition word for the author to use to connect these two sentences?**
   (Easy)

   Surprisingly enough, some spiders even live on water! The water spider lives in slow moving or still water.

   A.   Then,

   B.   Beyond,

   C.   For example,

   D.   Immediately,

Answer: C. For example,
"For example," would indicate that the author is going to offer an example as she has done in the paragraph. Therefore, it would have been the best transition word to use to connect the two sentences.

9. **What does the word *meander* mean in the sentence below?**
   (Easy)

   Michael was taking a long time to return to his seat after sharpening his pencil at the back of the room. After leaving the sharpener, he meandered around the room before eventually making his way back to his own seat.

   A.   rolled

   B.   roamed

   C.   slithered

   D.   stomped

Answer: B. roamed
The student *roamed* around the room before returning to his seat.

10. **What does the word *interject* mean in the sentence below?**
(Easy)

Nancy was speaking with her best friend Sierra. Nancy's little sister was standing nearby and was eavesdropping on their conversation. Suddenly, she heard something that interested her and had to <u>interject</u> her opinion about the subject the girls were talking about.

 A. repeat

 B. pierce

 C. intersect

 D. state

Answer: D. state
By *interjecting* her opinion, Nancy's little sister had to "state" her opinion, or make her idea known.

11. **When reading the book *Stormbreaker* by Anthony Horowitz the reader feels like they are a part of the action. The author uses so many details to bring the reader into the setting of story and this puts the reader right beside Alex Rider, the main character in the story.**

 Is this a valid or invalid argument?
 (Average)

 A. Valid

 B. Invalid

Answer: A. Valid
The argument is valid because there is support that backs up the argument that while reading *Stormbreaker*, the reader feels as if they are a part of the action.

12. Let's go see the movie *Alice in Wonderland.* It's a great movie and is Johnny Depp is awesome!

   Is this a valid or invalid argument?
   (Average)

   A.   Valid

   B.   Invalid

Answer: B. Invaild
The speaker does not offer any support for why they should go and see the movie *Alice in Wonderland* other than the fact that it's a great movie and Johnny Depp is awesome in it.

13. **Which sentence in the passage below is irrelevant?**
   (Rigorous)

   Davy Crockett grew up in Tennessee. When he was just a young boy he learned to hunt, fish, and drive cattle. At twelve years old, he traveled three hundred miles to complete a cattle drive. Davy's father thought school was important, but Davy did not agree. He left home and did not return until he was fifteen. He had grown to nearly six feet tall. When he returned, he was employed by a farmer whose son taught school. It was because of this fact that Davy developed a new interest in reading and writing. Davy also developed another interest—shooting rifles and hunting animals. He often missed his mother. Legend has it that Davy had very good aim and captured more than 100 bears in just a six-month period.

   A.   Davy Crockett grew up in Tennessee

   B.   When he was just a young boy he learned to hunt, fish, and drive cattle

   C.   He had grown to nearly six-feet tall

   D.   Legend has it that Davy had very good aim

Answer: C. He had grown to nearly six-feet tall
The fact that Davy had grown to nearly six feet tall is not necessary to the paragraph.

14. **Which sentence in the passage above is irrelevant?**
    (Rigorous)

    A.   Davy also developed another interest.

    B.   He often missed his mother.

    C.   Legend has it that Davy had very good aim.

    D.   Davy captured more than 100 bears in just six months.

Answer- B. He often missed his mother.
The idea that Davy often missed his mother does not fit in where it is in the paragraph—it is irrelevant.

15. **Boys are smarter than girls. Is this sentence fact or opinion?**
    (Easy)

    A.   Fact

    B.   Opinion

Answer: B. Opinion
There isn't any scientific evidence to back up this idea.

16. **Turkey burgers are better than beef burgers. Is this sentence fact or opinion?**
    (Easy)

    A.   Fact

    B.   Opinion

Answer: B. Opinion
Those that believe that turkey burgers are better than beef burgers might think this statement is a fact. However, it is not able to be proven and can in fact be argued so therefore, it is an opinion.

17. **Johnny Depp stars in the movie *Charlie and the Chocolate Factory*. Is this sentence fact or opinion?**
    (Easy)

    A.   Fact

    B.   Opinion

Answer: A. Fact
It can be proven that Johnny Depp is the actor that stars in *Charlie and the Chocolate Factory*.

18. **We live at 5310 Fair Oaks Drive in Chicago, Illinois. Is this sentence fact or opinion?**
    (Easy)

    A.   Fact

    B.   Opinion

Answer: A. Fact
The address that the author resides at is indisputable and cannot be argued. Therefore, it is a fact.

19. **What conclusion can be drawn from the passage below?**
    (Rigorous)

    When she walked into the room she gasped in disbelief as her hands rose to her face and her eyes bulged large. After she picked her jaw up off the floor, a huge smile spread across her face as her best friend came up and wrapped her arms around her and wished her a happy birthday.

    A.   The girl didn't know anyone in the room

    B.   The girl saw something shocking

    C.   The girl was being thrown a surprise party

    D.   The girl got punched in the face

Answer: C. The girl was being thrown a surprise party
The last sentence of the paragraph solidifies the idea that the girl is being thrown a surprise party for her birthday.

20. What conclusion can be drawn from the paragraph below?
(Average)

Joel stood at the water's edge staring into the waves as his legs trembled violently. His mind flashed back to last summer and his entire body joined his legs and began to tremble. He tried to even his breathing as he took slow deep breaths before deciding to head into the surf.

A.   The water was really cold

B.   Joel saw a shark in the water

C.   Last summer was better than this summer

D.   Joel is afraid of the water because something happened

Answer: D. Joel is afraid of the water because something happened
There are many clues that would lead to any of these choices. However, Joel is trembling with fear and thinks back to the summer before because something terrible must have happened.

Directions: Read the following passage and answer questions 21–24.

Deciding which animal to get as the family pet can be a very difficult decision and there are many things to take into consideration. First, you must consider the size of your home and the area that will be dedicated to the pet. If your home is a smaller one, then you probably want to get a small dog or even a cat. If you are lucky enough to have larger home with plenty of room inside and out, then most certainly consider a large or even a more active breed of dog. One other thing to is how often and how long you are outside of the home. Cats do not need to be let out to relieve themselves. They are normally trained to use a litter box. On the other hand, dogs require being let out. Dogs also require more exercise than cats and often need to be walked. This can be aggravating to an owner especially on rainy days. Therefore, when deciding which pet is best for your family, it is necessary to consider more than whether or not you want a dog or a cat, but which animal will best fit into your family's lifestyle.

21. How does the author feel about dogs?
(Rigorous)

A.   The author likes dogs and cats the same

B.   The author thinks that dogs are aggravating

C.   The author believes they require more care than cats

D.   The author feels that dogs are more active than cats

Answer: C: The author believes they require more care than cats
The author gives two examples of things dogs need rather than cats. It is stated that dogs require being let out and that they require more exercise.

22. How does the author feel about the size of people's houses?
(Rigorous)

A.   The author believes that people with larger homes are lucky

B.   The author thinks that if you have a small house you should have a cat

C.   The author feels that only people with large homes should own animals

D.   The author thinks that only those who own homes should own pets

Answer: A. The author believes that people with larger homes are lucky
Within the passage the author says, "If you are lucky enough to own a large house."

23. From this passage, one can infer that:
   (Rigorous)

   A   The author owns a cat

   B   More people own dogs than cats

   C   Cats are smarter than dogs

   D   The author owns a dog

Answer: D. The author owns a dog
One sentence in particular gives the reader the idea that the author owns a dog because she says, "This can be aggravating [letting a dog out] to an owner especially on rainy days."

24. From this passage, one can infer that:
   (Rigorous)

   A.   Either a dog or cat will be right for every family who wants a pet

   B.   Choosing a pet is not solely one family member's job

   C.   Only someone who enjoys exercising should get a dog

   D.   Big dogs will not survive in a small house

Answer: A. Either a dog or cat will be right for every family who wants a pet
The word "family" is used several times in the article, and therefore, the reader knows that choosing a pet is a family's responsibility—not just one member's.

Directions: Read the following passage and answer questions 25–31.

According to Factmonster.com, the most popular Internet activity is sending and/or reading email. Approximately 92% of Internet users report using the Internet for this purpose. 89% of Internet users report that they use the Internet to search for information. Two popular search engines are Google and Yahoo! The introduction of the Internet has made it easy to gather and research information quickly. Other reasons that Internet users use the Internet is to search for driving directions, look into a hobby or interest, or research a product or service before buying, just to name a few. Creative <u>enterprises</u> such as remixing songs or lyrics stood at the bottom of reasons people use the Internet. Surprisingly, only 11% of Internet users said they use the Internet for creative purposes. Perhaps people are using specific software to be creative. Where do you rank? Think about why you last used the Internet.

25. **What is the main idea of the passage?**
    (Average)

    A.   Factmonster has a lot of great facts for people to research

    B.   People use the Internet for a variety of reasons

    C.   The main reason the Internet is used is to check emails

    D.   People aren't as creative as they used to be before the Internet

Answer: B. People use the Internet for a variety of reasons
The passage lists the top reasons for why people use the Internet. Therefore, the best choice is Choice B.

26. **Why did the author write this article?**
    (Average)

    A.   To convince the reader to use the Internet

    B.   To teach the reader how use the Internet

    C.   To encourage the reader to use the Internet

    D.   To inform the reader about Internet usage trends

Answer: D. To inform the reader about Internet usage trends
The author wants to let the reader know what the Internet is mostly being used for. The statistics offered are synonymous of Internet usage trends.

27. **How is the passage above organized?**
    (Average)

    A.   Sequence of events

    B.   Cause and effect

    C.   Statement support

    D.   Compare and contrast

Answer: C. Statement support
The passage makes a statement at the beginning and then supports it with details in the rest of the passage.

28. **What cause and effect relationship exists in this paragraph?**
    (Rigorous)

    A.   The U.S. postal service is suffering from the introduction of email

    B.   Google and Yahoo! are used most often to search information

    C.   The introduction of the Internet has made gathering information easy

    D.   People are less creative since they aren't using their computers for this reason

Answer: C. The introduction of the Internet has made gathering information easy
Because the Internet was introduced, people are able to search for information easier than they used to be able to. This is a cause and effect relationship.

29. **By using the word *surprisingly* in the passage, what is the author implying?**
   (Rigorous)

   A.   It is thought that the Internet is used more creative purposes

   B.   People are thought to be more creative than they really are

   C.   It is thought that fewer than 11% would use the Internet for creative purposes

   D.   Software companies are making 11% more creative software

Answer: A. It is thought that the Internet is used more creative purposes
By using the word *surprisingly*, the author is saying that she is surprised that only 11% of Internet users use the Internet for creative purposes. The author would expect that number to be higher.

30. **Which transition word could the author have used to connect these two sentence?**
   (Average)

   Approximately 92% of Internet users report using the Internet for this purpose. 89% of Internet users report that they use the Internet to search for information.

   A.   Additionally,

   B.   Therefore,

   C.   Next,

   D.   Similarly,

Answer: A. Additionally,
The author wants to add more information about Internet usage so *additionally* is the best choice for a transition word.

31. **What does the word *enterprises* mean in the passage?**
    (Average)

      A.   people

      B.   endeavors

      C.   businesses

      D.   musicians

Answer: B. endeavors
The word endeavors and enterprises are synonymous, and either word could be used in the passage just the same.

Directions: Read the following passage and answer questions 32–34.

The poems both use personification to bring the subjects of the poem to life. Both poems were also very entertaining. In The Subway the author says that the subway, also known as a dragon, swallows up the people and then spits them out at the next stop. Similarly, in the poem Steam Shovel, the author says that the steam shovel chews up the dirt that it scoops up and smiles amiably at the people below.

      The subjects of the poems are compared to different things. The subway is compared to a dragon with green scales. Dragons breathe fire. The steam shovel is compared to an ancient dinosaur with a long neck and dripping jaws.

32. **How is the above passage organized?**
    (Average)

      A.   Compare and contrast

      B.   Cause and effect

      C.   Sequence of events

      D.   Statement support

Answer: A. Compare and contrast
This passage compares (gives similarities) and contrasts (shows differences) between two poems, The Subway and Steam Shovel.

33. **Which sentence in the passage above is irrelevant?**
    (Average)

    A.   Both poems were also very entertaining.

    B.   The subway is also known as a dragon.

    C.   The subway swallows people up and spits them out.

    D.   The author says that the steam shovel chews up the dirt.

Answer: A. Both poems were also very entertaining.
Although this may be a similarity between the two poems, it is an opinion and it is not necessary to include it within the passage since the focus of the first paragraph is personification.

34. **Which sentence in the passage above is irrelevant?**
    (Rigorous)

    A.   The subjects of the poems are compared to different things

    B.   The subway is compared to a dragon with green scales

    C.   Dragons breathe fire

    D.   The steam shovel is compared to an ancient dinosaur

Answer: C. Dragons breathe fire
Although "dragons breathe fire" is an extension of the idea that the subway is being compared to a dragon with green scales, the idea doesn't quite fit in well and isn't necessary.

Directions: Read the following passage and answer questions 35–36.

Have you ever wondered what chewing gum is made from? What it is that allows us to chew it for hours without ever disintegrating? Chicle is a gum, or sap, that comes from the sapodilla tree. The sapodilla tree is an American tropical evergreen that is native to South Florida. Flavorings, corn syrup, and sugar or artificial sweeteners are other ingredients that go into the production of chewing gum. Legend has it that Native Americans chewed spruce resin to quench their thirst. Today, gum is chewed for many reasons by many different groups of people.

35. **What conclusion can be drawn from the above passage?**
    (Rigorous)

    A.   Everyone in South Florida has heard of the sapodilla tree

    B.   Many people have wondered what makes gum chewy

    C.   Some type of sweetener is used in gum production

    D.   Native Americans invented gum

Answer: C. Some type of sweetener is used in gum production
It is defined in the passage that sugar or artificial sweeteners are used in gum production.

36. **What can be inferred from the passage?**
    (Rigorous)

    A.   The gum *Chiclets* took its name from the ingredient Chicle used in gum

    B.   Gum is disgusting after its been chewed for a few hours

    C.   Gum is only made in the United States because that's where the sapodilla tree grows

    D.   When someone is thirsty they should chew gum

Answer: A. The gum *Chiclets* took its name from the ingredient Chicle used in gum
It can be inferred from the passage that the brand of Chiclets gum most likely took its name from the ingredient Chicle, or sap, that is found in gum.

Directions: Read the following passage and answer questions 37–40.

The word *cycle* comes from the Greek word *kyklos*, which means circle or wheel. There are many different types of cycles. The word *unicycle* comes from the prefix *uni-*, which means "one," combined with the root *cycle*. When the prefix and root word cycle are combined, it creates a word that means one circle or wheel. Unicycles are often used for entertainment rather than exercise.

A suffix *bi-* means "two," which when combined with the word cycle, creates the word bicycle. How many wheels does a bicycle have? Many young children ride a tricycle because it has three wheels and is easy to ride. The prefix *tri-* means "three," and when it is combined with the root word *cycle* the new word is "three wheels." It is even possible to make the word *motorcycle.* Once you know how to use <u>roots</u>, it is easy to figure out the meaning of an unknown word.

37. **What is the main idea of the passage?**
    (Average)

    A.   There are many types of cycles

    B.   The prefix *uni-* means one

    C.   Words can be defined by its parts

    D.   Unicycles are often used for entertainment

Answer: C. Words can be defined by its parts
Only choice C covers the whole passage and not just one small detail contained within it.

38. **What does the word "roots" mean?**
    (Easy)

    A.   Stable parts of plants

    B.   Where one originated

    C.   The base portion of a word

    D.   A spelling tool

Answer: C. The base portion of a word
"Roots" is a multiple meaning word, but in the context of the passage, it means the base portion of a word.

39. Which is an opinion contained in this passage?
(Average)

A.   Once you know how to use roots, it is easy to figure out the meaning of an unknown word

B.   Many young children ride a tricycle

C.   Unicycles are often used for entertainment rather than exercise

D.   The word cycle comes from the Greek word *kyklos*

Answer: A. Once you know how to use roots, it is easy to figure out the meaning of an unknown word
Choices B and C could be opinions, but they both have clarifying words like "many" and "often," which makes them facts.

40. From this article you can see that the author thinks
(Rigorous)

A.   Riding a bicycle is good exercise

B.   It is important to know about the English language

C.   Cycle is a confusing word

D.   It is more important to understand the prefixes and suffixes

Answer: B. It is important to know about the English language
The author wrote this passage to teach readers about the English language. Therefore, we know that the author thinks it is important to understand the English language.

Answer Key: Reading

1.	B	21.	C
2.	D	22.	A
3.	A	23.	D
4.	C	24.	A
5.	D	25.	B
6.	B	26.	D
7.	C	27.	C
8.	C	28.	C
9.	B	29.	A
10.	D	30.	A
11.	A	31.	B
12.	B	32.	A
13.	C	33.	A
14.	B	34.	C
15.	B	35.	C
16.	B	36.	A
17.	A	37.	C
18.	A	38.	C
19.	C	39.	A
20.	D	40.	B

Rigor Table: Reading

	Easy 20%	Average 40%	Rigorous 40%
Questions	8, 9, 10, 15, 16, 17, 18, 38	1, 2, 4, 7, 11, 12, 20, 25, 26, 27, 30, 31, 32, 33, 37, 39	3, 5, 6, 13, 14, 15, 19, 21, 22, 23, 24, 28, 29, 34, 35, 36, 40

WRITING

Directions: Read the sentences and decide whether any of the underlined parts contains a grammatical construction, a word use, or an instance of incorrect or omitted punctuation or capitalization that would be inappropriate in carefully written English.

1. It will <u>definitely</u> be a great time and I am <u>positively</u> that everyone <u>who</u> attends will enjoy the party.
    (Average)

    A.   definite

    B.   positive

    C.   whom

    D.   No change is necessary

Answer: B. positive
Even though the sentence begins with the adverb "definitely," positively is the incorrect word to use later in the sentence.

2. There are <u>many</u> different <u>activities</u> planned for the day in all of the surrounding <u>communitys</u>.
    (Average)

    A.   much

    B.   activitys

    C.   communities

    D.   No change is necessary

Answer: C. communities
The word 'communities' is spelled incorrectly.

3. Jordan accepted <u>Chrises</u> invitation to go with him to the dance on Friday night.
   (Rigorous)

   A.   Chris's

   B.   Chris'

   C.   Chrises'

   D.   No change is necessary

Answer: A. Chris's
The sentence indicates possession—or Chris is the owner of the invitation. Therefore, an apostrophe is needed to show ownership.

4. Michelle <u>was trying</u> to do her homework, but <u>he was making</u> too much noise.
   (Rigorous)

   A.   tried

   B.   her brother

   C.   made

   D.   No change is necessary

Answer: B. her brother
The pronoun "he" cannot be used because the only noun that appears in the sentence so far is Michelle, and "he" cannot be the pronoun to take the place of Michelle. More clarification is needed as to who "he" is.

5. **When I returned home after running errands for the past hour, I wondered <u>whose</u> car was parked in my driveway.**
   (Rigorous)

   A.   who's

   B.   who is

   C.   whos

   D.   No change is necessary

Answer: D. No change is necessary
The word "whose" is the correct form of the word for this situation.

6. **The expectations that have been put on <u>teachers</u> in the past few years <u>have grown</u> and <u>they</u> are very difficult to manage.**
   (Rigorous)

   A.   teacher's

   B.   has grown

   C.   these expectations

   D.   No change is necessary

Answer: C. these expectations
The pronoun "they" is not clearly identified. It can be replacing either the teachers or the expectations. Clarification is needed, as in choice C, rather than simply using the pronoun "they."

7. Austin <u>was watching</u> television on the couch when his dad <u>looked</u> at him with an encouraging look. "I <u>has taken</u> out the trash already," Austin said.
   (Average)

   A.   had watched

   B.   looking

   C.   have taken

   D.   No change is necessary

Answer: C. have taken
The past participle of the verb to take is taken.

8. <u>Christian Montgomery</u> <u>our honorable mayor</u> will be leading us in the <u>ceremonies</u> that day.
   (Rigorous)

   A.   Chritian montgomery

   B.   Montgomery, our honorable mayor,

   C.   Ceremonies

   D.   No change is necessary

Answer: B. Montgomery, our honorable mayor,
Commas are needed to separate the dependent clause, our honorable mayor. We know this is a dependent clause because if it were removed from the sentence, the sentence would still make sense.

9. **Pizza tastes <u>more better</u> when you <u>put</u> <u>cheese</u>, mushrooms, and onions all over the top of it.**
   (Easy)

   A.   better

   B.   putt

   C.   cheesy

   D.   No change is necessary

Answer: A. better
More better is an incorrect adjective. The correct adjective needed is simply "better."

10. **The lemonade that <u>was being</u> sold at the <u>children's</u> lemonade stand was <u>more sweet</u> than the iced tea.**
    (Rigorous)

    A.   has been

    B.   childrens

    C.   sweeter

    D.   No change is necessary

Answer: C. sweeter
The correct word to use when comparing sweet items is "sweeter," not "more sweet." All of the other choices are correct in the sentence.

11. **The <u>students</u> and the <u>teachers</u> <u>is</u> going to attend the performance at noon on Thursday.**
(Easy)

    A.   student's

    B.   teachers'

    C.   are

    D.   No change is necessary

Answer: C. are
The linking verb agreement must correspond with the plurality of the subjects. The subjects are the students and the teachers; this is a compound subject. Therefore, "are" is needed to correspond with these subjects.

12. **After the town was evacuated <u>due to</u> expected strong <u>storms,</u> I reported to the authorities that there <u>wasn't nobody</u> left in our whole house.**
(Average)

    A.   because of

    B.   storms I...

    C.   wasn't anybody

    D.   No change is necessary

Answer: C. wasn't anybody
"Wasn't nobody" is a double negative and is an error. Two forms of negation cannot be used together in a sentence. The correct word to use with "wasn't" is "anybody"—choice C.

13. **This weekend we are going to <u>mow </u>the <u>lawn, wash</u> the windows and <u>trimming</u> the shrubs.**
   (Easy)

   A.   mowing

   B.   lawn; wash

   C.   trim

   D.   No change is necessary

Answer: C. trim
The sentence is in the future tense, "are going," and lists the things that need be done as, mow the lawn, and wash the windows. Therefore, the last item, trim the shrubs needs to stay parallel with the two items listed first.

14. **The local meteorologists <u>are</u> forecasting <u>neither</u> rain <u>or</u> snow for the holiday week.**
   (Rigorous)

   A.   is

   B.   niether

   C.   nor

   D.   No change is necessary

Answer: C. nor
The correlative conjunction neither is used. Therefore, when neither is used, nor must follow—not or. Or is used in correlation with the word either.

15. We will <u>be celebrating</u> the <u>Fourth of July</u> at <u>independence park</u> located in the center of Gorham Township.
    (Average)

    A.   celebrating

    B.   fourth of July

    C.   Independence Park

    D.   No change is necessary

Answer: C. Independence Park
Independence Park is the proper name of a specific park and therefore must be capitalized.

Directions: In each of the following sentences, some part of the sentence or the entire sentence is underlined. Beneath each sentence you will find four ways of writing the underlined part. Select the best answer that will make the sentence correct.

16. <u>The states of Oklahoma, Texas and Missouri were severe affected by the drought caused from a lack of rain this summer.</u>
    (Average)

    A.   The states of Oklahoma, Texas and Missouri were more severely affected by the drought caused from a lack of rain this summer.

    B.   The states of Oklahoma, Texas and Missouri was severely affected by the drought caused from a lack of rain this summer.

    C.   The states of Oklahoma, Texas and Missouri were severely affected by the drought caused from a lack of rain this summer.

    D.   No change is necessary

Answer: C. The states of Oklahoma, Texas and Missouri were severely affected by the drought caused from a lack of rain this summer.
The adverb "severely" is needed to describe how the three states were affected from the lack of rain this summer.

17. **Who do you think has the neatest handwriting in the class?**
    (Rigorous)

    A.   Whom do you think have the neater handwriting in the class?

    B.   Who do you think have the neatest handwriting in the class?

    C.   Who do you think has the neatest handwriting in the class.

    D.   No change is necessary

Answer: D. No change is necessary
The original sentence is written and punctuated correctly. No changes are needed. The statement is a question and therefore requires a question mark.

18. **The professor and his assistant presented they're report at the annual conference of financial economic stimulus representatives.**
    (Average)

    A.   The professor and his assistant presented its report at the annual conference of financial economic stimulus representatives.

    B.   The professor and his assistant presented theirs report at the annual conference of financial economic stimulus representatives.

    C.   The professor and his assistant presented their report at the annual conference of financial economic stimulus representatives.

    D.   No change is necessary

Answer: C. The professor and his assistant presented their report at the annual conference of financial economic stimulus representatives.
The report belongs to the professor and his assistant therefore the correct pronoun to use is "their."

19. **Since its supposed to rain today I think its best if you take your umbrella.**
(Average)

    A.   Since it's supposed to rain today, I think its best if you take you're umbrella.

    B.   Since it's supposed to rain today, I think it's best if you take your umbrella.

    C.   Since its supposed to rain today I think its best if you take you're umbrealla.

    D.   No change is necessary

Answer: B. Since it's supposed to rain today, I think it's best if you take your umbrella.
There were three words to examine closely in this sentence: "its," "its," and "your." "It's" is the contraction for the two words it + is. "Its" shows possession. "You're" is the contraction for the two words you + are. If the contraction does not work in the sentence, for example, "take *you are* umbrella," then the contraction is not grammatically correct.

20. **Our regularly scheduled meeting will be hold on Tuesday, March 11 at 3:00 that afternoon.**
(Easy)

    A.   Our regular scheduled meeting will be hold on Tuesday, March 11 at 3:00 in the afternoon.

    B.   Our regularly scheduled meeting will be held on Tuesday, March 11 at 3:00 in the afternoon.

    C.   Are regularly scheduled meeting will be held on Tuesday, March 11 at 3:00 that afternoon.

    D.   No change is necessary

Answer: B. Our regularly scheduled meeting will be held on Tuesday, March 11 at 3:00 in the afternoon.
The word hold needs to be "held" because of the way the sentence is worded. If it were, "We will *hold* our regularly scheduled meeting..." then the verb would have to be "hold" to indicate the future tense.

21. **The frog eggs were laid a few weeks ago, so they have been hatching soon.**
(Easy)

   A.   The frog eggs were laid a few weeks ago, so they will be hatching soon.

   B.   The frog eggs were laid a few weeks ago, so they is hatching soon.

   C.   The frog eggs were laid a few weeks ago, so they be done hatching soon.

   D.   No change is necessary

Answer: A. The frog eggs were laid a few weeks ago, so they will be hatching soon.
The correct future tense form of the verb that is needed is will be hatching soon.

22. **We were supposed to work on a project for school, but after an hour we started to get hungry and deciding to make popcorn.**
(Average)

   A.   We were supposed to work on a project for school, but after an hour we started to get hungry and were deciding to make popcorn.

   B.   We were supposed to work on a project for school, but after an hour we started to get hungry and dedide to make popcorn.

   C.   We were supposed to work on a project for school, but after an hour we started to get hungry and decided to make popcorn.

   D.   No change is necessary

Answer: C. We were supposed to work on a project for school, but after an hour we started to get hungry and decided to make popcorn.
The sentence is written in the past tense and therefore must remain in the past tense. Therefore, the verb "decided" is needed to make the sentence grammatically correct.

23. **I had brought home some movies from the video store but not anybody wanted to watch them so we played a game instead.**
   (Average)

   A.   I brought home some movies from the video store but not anyone wanted to watch them so we played a game instead.

   B.   I brought home some movies from the video store but nobody wanted to watch them so we played a game instead.

   C.   I brought home some movies from the video store but somebody wanted to watch them so we played a game instead.

   D.   No change is necessary

Answer: B. I brought home some movies from the video store but nobody wanted to watch them so we played a game instead.
All of the sentences contain double negatives except choice B. The correct term is "nobody."

24. **Coloring hard boiled eggs is an Easter tradition that many people still follow today.**
   (Rigorous)

   A.   that many people followed today

   B.   that many people following today

   C.   that much peoples follow today

   D.   No change is necessary

Answer: D. No change is necessary
The way the sentence is written is correct and no changes are necessary.

25. **Temperatures are rising, <u>yet the trees are blooming and the grass is quickly growing</u>.**
    (Rigorous)

    A.   but the trees is blooming and the grass is quickly growing

    B.   and the trees are blooming and the grass is quickly growing

    C.   yet, the trees are blooming and the grass is quickly growing

    D.   No change is necessary

Answer: B. and the trees are blooming and the grass is quickly growing
This is a cause and effect sentence. Because the temperatures are rising, the trees are blooming and the grass is quickly growing. Therefore, a connecting word like "and" is needed rather than a contradictory word like "but" or "yet."

26. **<u>In my opinion we would all be much better off if there were less choices in the grocery stores.</u> There seems to be an overabundance of choice and it is confusing to some.**
    (Rigorous)

    A.   In my opinion, we should all be much more better off is there was less choices in the grocery stores.

    B.   In my opinion, we would all be better off if there were less choices in the grocery stores.

    C.   In my opinion we would all be much better off if there were fewer choices in the grocery stores.

    D.   No change is necessary

Answer: C. In my opinion we would all be much better off if there were fewer choices in the grocery stores.
The only word that must be changed in the original sentence is "less" to "fewer." "Less" is used to answer the question, "How much?" whereas "fewer" is used to answer the question, "How many?"

27. **Supposably, the keynote speaker at the annual convention is an alumni of Princeton University.**
   (Average)

   A.   Supposedly, the keynote speaker at the annual convention is an alumni of Princeton University.

   B.   Supposably the keynote speaker, at the annual convention, is an alumni of Princeton University.

   C.   Supposably, the keynote speaker during the annual convention was an alumnus at Princeton University.

   D.   No change is necessary

Answer: A. Supposedly, the keynote speaker at the annual convention is an alumni of Princeton University.
All of the other choices are automatically incorrect, because "supposably" is incorrect. The correct word is "supposedly."

28. **I was not expecting to except his advice but it actually made sense and solved the problem.**
   (Rigorous)

   A.   I was not expecting to except his advise, but it actually made sense and solved the problem.

   B.   I was not expecting to accept his advice but it actually made sense and solved the problem.

   C.   I was not expecting to except his advice since it actually made sense and solved the problem.

   D.   No change is necessary

Answer: B. I was not expecting to accept his advice but it actually made sense and solved the problem.
The only problem with the original sentence is the word "except," which means "excluding." This sentence calls for the word "accept" which means "to receive or to tolerate."

29. **When children are learning to read, they often read allowed in order to assist with monitoring their own comprehension.**
    (Average)

    A.   When children is learning to read, we often read allowed in order to assist with monitoring their own comprehension.

    B.   When children are learning to read, they often read aloud in order to assist with monitoring their own comprehension.

    C.   When children are learning to read, she often read allowed in order to assist with monitor there own comprehension.

    D.   No change is necessary

Answer: B. When children are learning to read, they often read aloud in order to assist with monitoring their own comprehension.
The only error in the original sentence is with the word "allowed." Allowed means permitted. The word needed here is "aloud," which is an adverb that means audible or able to be heard.

30. **Many northern residents are choosing to immigrate to the south to take advantage of lower taxes and nicer weather.**
    (Rigorous)

    A.   Many Northern residents are choosing to immigrate to the South to take advantage of lower taxes and nicer weather.

    B.   Many northern residents choosed to immigrate to the south to take advantage of lower taxes and nicer weather.

    C.   Many northern residents are choosing to emigrate to the south to take advantage of lower taxes and nicer weather.

    D.   No change is necessary

Answer: C. Many northern residents are choosing to emigrate to the south to take advantage of lower taxes and nicer weather.
The only error in the original sentence is the word "immigrate," which means "to enter another country and reside there." In this sentence, residents are leaving and settling in another region, which is "emigrate."

31. **When I was younger, my family and I used to go to visit my grandparents for the summer at their home in North Carolina.** *(Rigorous)*

    A.   When I was younger, my family and I use to go to visit my grandparents for the summer at their home in North Carolina.

    B.   When I was younger, my family and me used to go to visit my Grandparent's for the summer at their home in North Carolina.

    C.   When I was younger my family and us used to go to visit my grandparents for the summer at there home in North Carolina.

    D.   No change is necessary

Answer: D. No change is necessary
The sentence is correct the way it is written but there are many places to check. First, the correct wording is "used to." Next, "my family and I" is written correctly. A way to check is to delete "my family" and try the sentence that way. "I used to go... me used to go..." Choose the one that is grammatically correct. Finally, the correct form need is "their" home since it shows possession.

32. <u>**Maurice put together a good presentation in class and he did good.**</u> *(Average)*

    A.   Maurice put together a good presentation in class and he did well.

    B.   Maurice put together a well presentation in class and he did well.

    C.   Maurice put together a well presentation in class and he did good.

    D.   No change is necessary

Answer: A. Maurice put together a good presentation in class and he did well.
Describing the presentation requires the word "good." However, when describing the effort level someone has shown, the word "well" is needed.

33. I can't believe that you didn't see that red light that was so oblivious.
(Easy)

A.   I can't believe that you didn't see that red light that was so enormous.

B.   I can't believe that you didn't see that red light that was so relevant.

C.   I can't believe that you didn't see that red light that was so obvious.

D.   No change is necessary

Answer: C. I can't believe that you didn't see that red light that was so obvious.
The correct word here to be used is "obvious," which means unable to go unnoticed.

34. My lunchbox contained many different treats; cookies, fruit, nuts, and cheese.
(Rigorous)

A.   My lunchbox contained many different treats: cookies, fruit, nuts, and cheese.

B.   My lunchbox contained many different treats, cookies, fruit, nuts and cheese.

C.   My lunchbox contained many different treats. cookies, fruit, nuts and cheese.

D.   No change is necessary

Answer: A. My lunchbox contained many different treats: cookies, fruit, nuts, and cheese.
The correct punctuation mark to use before a series of items listed and separated by commas is the colon. In addition, a comma is required between the words "nuts" and "cheese" because there are items listed in a series.

35. <u>Under the bridge near the river bank many turtles sat sunning themselves.</u>
(Average)

A.   Under the bridge near the river bank, much turtles sat sunny theirselves.

B.   Under the bridge, near the river bank, many turtles sat sunning themselves.

C.   Under the bridge near the river bank, many turtles sat sunning themselves.

D.   No change is necessary

Answer: C. Under the bridge near the river bank, many turtles sat sunning themselves.
The dependent clause "Under the bridge near the river bank" requires a comma afterward. "Many" is used to describe the number of turtles because they could be counted. Also, "themselves" is the correct word.

36. <u>I have just finished the book, "The Lion king," and I would recommend it to anyone who enjoys a good mystery.</u>
(Average)

A.   I have just finished the book *The Lion King* and I would recommend it to anyone who enjoys a good mystery.

B.   I have just finished the book *the Lion King* and I would recommend it to anyone who enjoys a good mystery.

C.   I have just finished the book, "the lion king" and I would recommend it to anyone who enjoys a good mystery.

D.   No change is necessary

Answer: A. I have just finished the book *The Lion King* and I would recommend it to anyone who enjoys a good mystery.
The rule is that if a title is typed, then it should be in italics. If a title is handwritten, it should be underlined. In addition, each word of the title must be capitalized.

37. **The rabbit was named kangaroo because it liked to jump.**
   (Average)

   A.   The Rabbit was named Kangaroo because it liked to jump.

   B.   The rabbit was named Kangaroo because it liked to jump.

   C.   The Rabbit was named kangaroo because it liked to jump.

   D.   No change is necessary

Answer: B. The rabbit was named Kangaroo because it liked to jump.
The rabbit's name is Kangaroo and proper nouns must be capitalized.

38. **The documentary that we watched about the battle of bull run was very graphic.**
   (Easy)

   A.   The documentary that we watched about the battle of Bull Run was very graphic.

   B.   The documentary that we watched about the battle of Bull run was very graphic.

   C.   The documentary that we watched about The Battle of Bull Run was very graphic.

   D.   No change is necessary

Answer: A. The documentary that we watched about the battle of Bull Run was very graphic.
Bull Run is the place where the battle took place and is therefore a proper noun and requires both words to be capitalized.

Answer Key: Writing

1.	B	20.	B
2.	C	21.	A
3.	A	22.	C
4.	B	23.	B
5.	D	24.	D
6.	C	25.	B
7.	C	26.	C
8.	B	27.	A
9.	A	28.	B
10.	C	29.	B
11.	C	30.	C
12.	C	31.	D
13.	C	32.	A
14.	C	33.	C
15.	C	34.	A
16.	C	35.	C
17.	D	36.	A
18.	C	37.	B
19.	B	38.	A

Rigor Table: Writing

	Easy 18.4%	Average 42.1%	Rigorous 39.5%
Questions	9,11,13, 20, 21, 33, 38,	1, 2, 7, 12, 15, 16, 18, 19, 22, 23, 27, 29, 32, 35, 36, 37	3, 4, 5, 6, 8, 10, 14, 17, 24, 25, 26, 28, 30, 31, 34,

Writing Essay

"Because the traditional grading scale of A through F fosters needless competition and pressure, colleges and universities should use a simple pass/fail system."

Discuss the extent to which you agree or disagree with this opinion. Support your views with specific reasons and examples from your own experience, observations, or reading.

Sample Score 5

I completely disagree with the idea that traditional grading scales foster needless competition and pressure, and colleges and universities should not use a simple pass/fail system. The reason I so strongly disagree with this idea is because I think that competition is healthy and is being stolen from our lives, and we are not becoming better producers because of it.

When I was younger, I remember field day. During field day, each class of students competed against each other in events such as the three-legged race, the 50-yard dash, the mixed relay etc. At the end of the day, 1st, 2nd, and 3rd place ribbons were awarded to the classes that earned each ribbon. Today, schools have field day, but they do not really "compete" against each other. At the end of the day, everyone is a winner who has participated in the events. This is not the way real life is. Real life is competitive.

If colleges simply had a pass/fail system, students would be even less prepared for the real world. Students would be lumped into only two categories—pass or fail. I feel that students would not learn the importance of competition and they would not be able to stand out nor learn how to stand out. Employers would not have a way to evaluate their future employees, and we would all just be "the same." As a teacher and a parent, I like to teach my students and children that we all have special gifts. Some of us are gifted in athletics while others are gifted in academics. Some are gifted in music, while others are gifted artists. If we were all lumped into only two categories, we would never discover our true talents.

Having only two scales—pass/fail—would not prepare students for what the real world holds in the future.

Sample score 2

Having a pass/fail grading scale is a bad idea. Growing up, there was competition during field days. This helped myself and the people I grew up with become prepared for the competitive future that we are all involved in now. It helped us to know how to stand out and be unique. This is an important quality to be able to succeed these days in the competitive business world.

If we were all lumped into only two categories—pass/fail—then employers would not be able to identify the best of the best or those that stood out and were unique. We wouldn't have anything to strive for because we would all just want to pass. By using an A through F grading scale, we are able to strive to be the best if we choose to. Employers are then able to tell who are indeed the best of the best.

MATH

1. **Express .0000456 in scientific notation.**
   (Average)

   A. $4.56x10^{-4}$

   B. $45.6x10^{-6}$

   C. $4.56x10^{-6}$

   D. $4.56x10^{-5}$

Answer: D. $4.56x10^{-5}$
In scientific notation, the decimal point belongs to the right of the 4, the first significant digit. To get from 4.56×10^{-5} back to 0.0000456, we would move the decimal point 5 places to the left.

2. **Change $.\overline{63}$ into a fraction in simplest form.**
   (Rigorous)

   A. $63/100$

   B. $7/11$

   C. $6\ 3/10$

   D. $2/3$

Answer: B. 7/11
Let N = .636363…. Then, multiplying both sides of the equation by 100 or 10^2 (because there are 2 repeated numbers), we get 100N = 63.636363… Then subtracting the two equations (N = .636363… and 100N = 63.636363…), gives 99N = 63 or N = $\dfrac{63}{99} = \dfrac{7}{11}$.

3. **The digit 4 in the number 302.41 is in the**
   (Easy)

   A.   Tenths place

   B.   Ones place

   C.   Hundredths place

   D.   Hundreds place

Answer: A. Tenths place

4. **Which of the following illustrates an inverse property?**
   (Easy)

   A. $a + b = a - b$

   B. $a + b = b + a$

   C. $a + 0 = a$

   D. $a + (-a) = 0$

Answer: D. $a + (-a) = 0$
Because $a + (-a) = 0$ is a statement of the Additive Inverse Property of Algebra.

5. **$7t - 4 \cdot 2t + 3t \cdot 4 \div 2 =$**
   (Average)

   A. $5t$

   B. 0

   C. $31t$

   D. $18t$

Answer: A. $5t$
Using the order of operations, first perform multiplication and division from left to right; $7t - 8t + 6t$, then add and subtract from left to right.

6. **If cleaning costs are $32 for 4 hours, how much is it for 10.5 hours?**
   (Average)

   A. $112.50

   B. $87

   C. $84

   D. $76.50

Answer: C. $84
The hourly rate is $8 per hour, so 8 x 10.5 = $84.

7. **Estimate the sum of 1498 + 1309.**
   (Average)

   A.   2900

   B.   2850

   C.   2800

   D.   2600

Answer: C. 2800
As this is an estimate, you add 1500 and 1300 to get 2800.

8. **Mr. Brown feeds his cat premium cat food, which costs $40 per month. Approximately how much will it cost to feed her for one year?**
   (Average)

   A. $500

   B. $400

   C. $80

   D. $4800

Answer: A. $500
12(40) = 480, which is closest to $500

9. **A carton of milk priced at $6.00 is 30% off. Another carton priced at $5.80 is 20% off. Which one is the better buy?**
   (Rigorous)

   A.   The $5.80 carton

   B.   The $6.00 carton

   C.   Both are equal

   D.   There is not enough information

Answer: B. The $6.00 carton
The sale price of the $6.00 carton = $6.00 \times 0.7 = \$4.20$; the sale price of the $5.80 carton = $\$5.80 \times 0.8 = \$4.64$. Hence, the $6.00 carton is the better buy.

10. **What is 30% of 450?**
    (Easy)

    A.   120

    B.   135

    C.   115

    D.   None of the above

Answer: B. 135

The percentage is given by $\dfrac{30}{100} \times 450 = 135$.

11. Joe reads 20 words/min., and Jan reads 80 words/min. How many minutes will it take Joe to read the same number of words that it takes Jan 40 minutes to read?
(Rigorous)

A. 10

B. 20

C. 80

D. 160

Answer: D. 160

If Jan reads 80 words/minute, she will read 3200 words in 40 minutes. Assume that Joe reads 3200 words in x minutes and set up a proportion relationship:

$$\frac{20}{1} = \frac{3200}{x}$$

Cross-multiplying, 20x = 3200; x = 3200/20 = 160.

12. Which of the following is a simple statement that can be assigned a truth value?
(Average)

A. It is sunny today

B. Please put away the books

C. The wind blew and the leaves fell

D. They will stay home or they will go to the mall

Answer: A. It is sunny today

The statement in choice B cannot be assigned a truth value. Choices C and D are compound statements formed by joining simple statements using the connectives "and" and "or."

13. **The following is an example of reasoning using:**

   They drove or they rode the bus.
   They did not drive, therefore they rode the bus.
   (Average)

   A.   Law of detachment

   B.   Law of contraposition

   C.   Law of syllogism

   D.   Disjunctive syllogism

Answer: D. Disjunctive syllogism
Disjunctive syllogism is of the form: p or q. Not p, therefore q.

14. **Solve for x:**

   3x + 5 ≥ 8 + 7x

   (Average)

   A. $x \geq -\dfrac{3}{4}$

   B. $x \leq -\dfrac{3}{4}$

   C. $x \geq \dfrac{3}{4}$

   D. $x \leq \dfrac{3}{4}$

Answer: B. $x \leq -\dfrac{3}{4}$
Using additive equality, -3 ≥ 4x. Divide both sides by 4 to obtain -3/4 ≥ x.

15. **Solve for x:**

$7 + 3x - 6 = 3x + 5 - x$

(Average)

   A.   2.5

   B.   4

   C.   4.5

   D.   27

Answer: B. 4
$7 + 3x - 6 = 3x + 5 - x$; $7 - 6 = 5 - x$; $-x = 1 - 5 = -4$; $x = 4$.

16. **Marvin bought a bag of candy. He gave half of the pieces to his friend Mike and one-third of the pieces to his sister Lisa. He ate half of the remaining pieces and had 15 left. How many pieces of candy were in the bag in the beginning?**
(Rigorous)

   A.   120

   B.   90

   C.   30

   D.   180

Answer: D. 180
Let the original number of pieces of candy in the bag be x. Mike got x/2 pieces of candy and Lisa got x/3 pieces. The number of pieces left =

$$x - \frac{x}{2} - \frac{x}{3} = \frac{6x}{6} - \frac{3x}{6} - \frac{2x}{6} = \frac{x}{6}$$

After Marvin ate half the remaining pieces x/12 pieces were left. Since x/12 = 15, the original number of pieces x = 12 x 15 = 180.

17. A boat travels 30 miles upstream in three hours. It makes the return trip in one and a half hours. What is the speed of the boat in still water? (Rigorous)

A. 10 mph

B. 15 mph

C. 20 mph

D. 30 mph

Answer: B. 15 mph

Let x = the speed of the boat in still water and c = the speed of the current.

	rate	time	distance
upstream	$x - c$	3	30
downstream	$x + c$	1.5	30

Solve the system:

$$3x - 3c = 30$$
$$1.5x + 1.5c = 30$$

Multiply the 2nd equation by 2, $3x + 3c = 60$; add the two equations, $6x = 90$; and solve for x.

$$x = 90/6 = 15$$

18. What is the next term in the sequence

$$\frac{2}{7}, \frac{13}{21}, \frac{20}{21}, \frac{9}{7}, \dots$$

(Rigorous)

A. $\frac{29}{21}$

B. $\frac{17}{21}$

C. $\frac{11}{7}$

D. $\frac{34}{21}$

Answer: D. $\frac{34}{21}$

This is an arithmetic sequence where each term is obtained by adding the common difference 7/21 or 1/3 to the preceding term. Thus the next term in the sequence is 9/7 + 1/3 = 34/21.

19. What is the 10th term in the following sequence?

    3, 6, 12, 24, …..

(Rigorous)

A.   3072

B.   1024

C.   512

D.   1536

Answer: D. 1536

This is a geometric sequence where each term is obtained by multiplying the previous term by 2. Hence the tenth term = 3 x 2^9 = 1536.

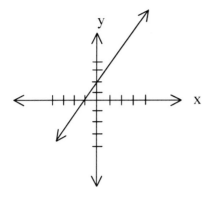

20. **What is the equation of the above graph?**
    (Average)

    A. $2x + y = 2$

    B. $2x - y = -2$

    C. $2x - y = 2$

    D. $2x + y = -2$

Answer: B. $2x - y = -2$

By observation, we see that the graph has a y-intercept of 2 and a slope of 2/1 = 2. Therefore its equation is y = mx + b = 2x + 2. Rearranging the terms gives 2x − y = -2.

21. **The figure below represents the position (x), velocity (v) and acceleration (a) of a car moving in one direction as functions of time (t). According to the graph**

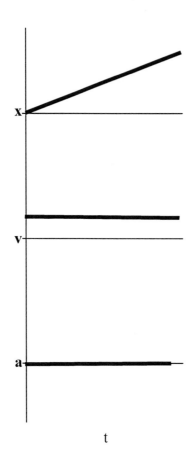

t

(Average)

A.   The car is at rest

B.   The car is moving at a fixed speed

C.   The car is speeding up

D.   The car changes direction in the middle

Answer: B. The car is moving at a fixed speed
Since the acceleration is zero, the velocity is constant and non-zero, and the position is changing, the car is moving at a fixed speed.

22. Which of the following shapes is a rhombus?
(Easy)

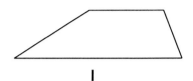

I

II

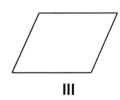

III

    A.   III

    B.   II

    C.   I

    D.   None of the above

Answer: A. III
A rhombus is a parallelogram with four equal sides.

23. **The angles in any triangle**
     (Easy)

    A.   Add up to 180 degrees

    B.   Are all equal

    C.   Are all right angles

    D.   Don't always add up to 180 degrees

Answer: A. Add up to 180 degrees

24. **If a ship sails due south 6 miles, then due west 8 miles, how far was it from the starting point?**
     (Average)

    A.   100 miles

    B.   10 miles

    C.   14 miles

    D.   48 miles

Answer: B. 10 miles
Draw a right triangle with legs of 6 and 8. Then, find the hypotenuse using the Pythagorean Theorem. $6^2 + 8^2 = c^2$. Therefore, c = 10 miles.

25. **A car is driven north at 74 miles per hour from point A. Another car is driven due east at 65 miles per hour starting from the same point at the same time. How far are the cars away from each other after 2 hours?**
    (Rigorous)

    A.   175.87 miles

    B.   232.66 miles

    C.   196.99 miles

    D.   202.43 miles

Answer: C. 196.99 miles
The route the cars take form a right triangle with edges 74 x 2 and 65 x 2. This gives two sides of a right triangle of 148 and 130. Using the Pythagorean Theorem, we get $148^2 + 130^2 = distance^2$. Therefore, the distance between the cars is 196.99.

26. **The mass of a cookie is closest to**
    (Average)

    A.   0.5 kg

    B.   0.5 grams

    C.   15 grams

    D.   1.5 grams

Answer: C. 15 grams
In terms of commonly used U.S. units, 15 grams is about half an ounce and 0.5 Kg is about a pound.

27. **You have a gallon of water and remove a total of 30 ounces. How many milliliters do you have left?**
   (Rigorous)

   A.   2900 ml

   B.   1100 ml

   C.   980 ml

   D.   1000 ml

Answer: A. 2900 ml
1 gallon = 128 fluid ouces. If 30 ounces are removed, you have 98 ounces left. Since 1 fluid ounce = 29.6 ml, 98 ounces = 2900 ml.

28. **Seventh grade students are working on a project using non-standard measurement. Which would not be an appropriate instrument for measuring the length of the classroom?**
   (Easy)

   A.   a student's foot

   B.   a student's arm span

   C.   a student's jump

   D.   all are appropriate

Answer: C. a student's jump
While a student's foot or student's arm span has a fixed length, a student's jump can vary in length and would therefore not be an appropriate unit.

29.

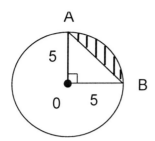

Compute the area of the shaded region, given a radius of 5 meters. 0 is the center.
(Rigorous)

A.   7.13 cm²

B.   7.13 m²

C.   78.5 m²

D.   19.63 m²

Answer: B. 7.13 m²

The area of triangle AOB is .5(5) (5) = 12.5 square meters. Since $\dfrac{90}{360} = .25$, the area of sector AOB (pie-shaped piece) is approximately $.25(\pi)5^2 = 19.63$. Subtracting the triangle area from the sector area to get the area of the shaded region, we get approximately 19.63-12.5 = 7.13 square meters.

30. Find the area of the figure pictured below.

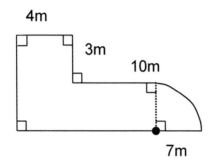

4m

3m

10m

7m

(Rigorous)

A.   136.47 m²

B.   148.48 m²

C.   293.86 m²

D.   178.47 m²

Answer: B. 148.48 m²
Divide the figure into 2 rectangles and one quarter circle. The tall rectangle on the left will have dimensions 10 by 4 and an area of 40. The rectangle in the center will have dimensions 7 by 10 and an area of 70. The quarter circle will have area $.25(\pi)7^2 = 38.48$. The total area is therefore approximately 148.48.

31. What conclusion can be drawn from the graph below?

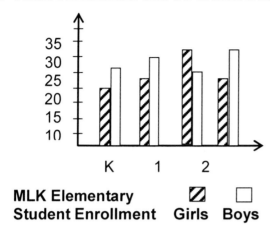

MLK Elementary
Student Enrollment   Girls   Boys

(Average)

A.   The number of students in first grade exceeds the number in second grade

B.   There are more boys than girls in the entire school

C.   There are more girls than boys in the first grade

D.   Third grade has the largest number of students

Answer: B. There are more boys than girls in the entire school
In kindergarten, first grade, and third grade, there are more boys than girls. The number of extra girls in grade two is more than made up for by the extra boys in all the other grades put together.

32. A school band has 200 members. Looking at the pie chart below, determine which statement is true about the band.

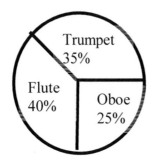

(Average)

A.   There are more trumpet players than flute players

B.   There are fifty oboe players in the band

C.   There are forty flute players in the band

D.   One-third of all band members play the trumpet

Answer: B. There are fifty oboe players in the band.
25% of 200 is 50.

33. **You wish to create a visual display showing test score trends over several decades for a school. What kind of chart would be the most suitable?**
(Average)

A.   circle graph

B.   bar graph

C.   histogram

D.   line graph

Answer: D. line graph
A line graph with the years plotted along the horizontal axis would be the best visual display of trends.

34. Which of the following statements is not true about the graph shown below?

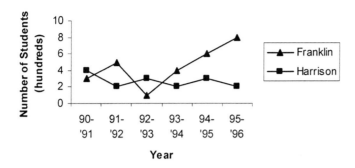

(Average)

A.   Franklin school shows a rising trend in student enrollment

B.   Harrison school shows a falling trend in student enrollment

C.   Both schools show similar trends in student enrollment

D.   Neither school has had more than 900 students

Answer is C. Both schools show similar trends in student enrollment

35. The stem and leaf plot below shows the heights of several children in a class in feet. What is the median height?
    (Easy)

3	6 9
4	1 2 3 4 4 9
5	1 3 5

A.   4 ft

B.   4.9 ft

C.   4.4 ft

D.   5.1 ft

Answer is C. 4.4 ft

36. **Which of these statements about the following data set is correct?**

2, 5, 12, 6, 3, 9, 5, 12, 20, 2, 3, 5, 21, 12

(Rigorous)

A.   There are 2 modes, the median is 8.5 and the range is 10

B.   There are 2 modes, the median is 5.5 and the range is 19

C.   There are 4 modes, the median is 5.5 and the range is 19

D.   There are 2 modes, the median is 5.5 and the range is 10

Answer: B. There are 2 modes, the median is 5.5 and the range is 19
The two modes are 5 and 12, since they each occur 3 times.

37. **Compute the median for the following data set:**

{12, 19, 13, 16, 17, 14}

(Easy)

A.   14.5

B.   15.17

C.   15

D.   16

Answer: C. 15
Arrange the data in ascending order: 12,13,14,16,17,19. The median is the middle value in a list with an odd number of entries. When there is an even number of entries, the median is the mean of the two center entries. Here the average of 14 and 16 is 15.

38. **How many ways are there to choose a potato and two green vegetables from a choice of three potatoes and seven green vegetables?**
   (Rigorous)

   A.   126

   B.   63

   C.   21

   D.   252

Answer: B. 63
There are 3 ways to choose a potato and the number of ways to choose 2 green vegetables from 7 is given by $\dfrac{7!}{5!2!} = 21$. Hence the total number of choices = 3 x 21 = 63.

39. **How many 3 letter sequences can be formed if the first letter must always be a consonant (not a, e, i, o , u), the second letter must always be a vowel (a, e, i, o, or u), and the third letter must be different from the first.**
   (Rigorous)

   A.   2100

   B.   4056

   C.   3250

   D.   2625

Answer: D. 2625
There are 21 choices for the first letter, 5 choices for the second letter, and 25 choices for the third letter. Hence, the number of possible sequences =
21 x 5 x 25 = 2625

40. Given a spinner with the numbers one through eight, what is the probability that you will not spin an even number or a number greater than four?
(Rigorous)

A. ¼

B. ½

C. ¾

D. 1

Answer: A. ¾
There are 8 possible outcomes. Of those, there are four even numbers 2, 4, 6, 8 and two other numbers (5 and 6) that are greater than 4. So six of the outcomes are even numbers or numbers greater than four. Hence, there are just two outcomes (1 and 3) that are neither even nor greater then four. Thus the probability that you will not spin an even number or a number greater than four is 2 out of 8, i.e. ¼.

Answer Key: Mathematics

1.	D	21.	B
2.	B	22.	A
3.	A	23.	A
4.	D	24.	B
5.	A	25.	C
6.	C	26.	C
7.	C	27.	A
8.	A	28.	C
9.	B	29.	B
10.	B	30.	B
11.	D	31.	B
12.	A	32.	B
13.	D	33.	D
14.	B	34.	C
15.	B	35.	C
16.	D	36.	B
17.	B	37.	C
18.	D	38.	B
19.	D	39.	D
20.	B	40.	A

Rigor Table: Mathematics

	Easy 20%	Average 42.5%	Rigorous 37.5%
Questions	3, 4, 10, 22, 23, 28, 35, 37	1, 5, 6, 7, 8, 12, 13, 14, 15, 20, 21, 24, 26, 31, 32, 33, 34	2, 9, 11, 16, 17, 18, 19, 25, 27, 29, 30, 36, 38, 39, 40

CPSIA information can be obtained at www.ICGtesting.com
Printed in the USA
BVOW050753150113

310644BV00006B/253/P

9 781607 872221